There IS ONLY ONE KIND OF SPECIAL AND That IS You

Hello, I Am LINDSEY

Written and Illustrated By Elena Pepitone

D1518586

DEDICATION

For my mom, Roberta, your beautiful heart will forever be my guiding treasure. Thank you will never be enough for every ounce of love, patience, and hug you gave me. Someday, I will be able to give back to you with everything I have. This book is a testament to everything you taught me, fought for, and everything you have had to sacrifice to provide with a special life. You will forever be my beautiful rainbow, always glowing more beautiful as only a beautiful angel can. I love you with every fiber of my being, Mom. You will forever be my inspiration.

Too all of you, throughout my life, you have inspired me more than you could possibly imagine. I was thinking of all of you, as I was writing this, and all you've given me. My heart is swollen by your love and strength, you each hold a special place in my heart. My rainbow has become more beautiful because of you. Lastly, for all the children, you inspire me more than you will ever know. May you fly your rainbow, and let it carry you as far as you want to go. Be brave, be true, Be You! You are all beautiful and amazing. I love you all so much. Thank you.

Lindsey Crickethopper could not wait to put her clothes on backwards. "Shirt and pants on inside out, *Check*! Socks that don't match, *Check*! Rainbow wig, *Check!* Super Excited, *Check!"* Lindsey's mom helped with on her makeup. "You look beautiful!" Mom said, proudly. "Hurry, Mom, I'm going to be late!" Lindsey said, rushing to put on her rainbow shoes. Lindsey couldn't wait for school to begin because it's the best school ever, "The Clown Academy."

YAY

LINDSEY

WEE

Butterfly

Butterfly

Lindsey
Looking
Happy

Swing

monkeys
Bars

Super
Wee!

Girl holding
Flower

ICE
Cream
Truck

Yay!
Ice
Cream!

The Clown
Acedemy

Super Etmer
On the Slide

5

This school is all about "FUN" and discovering the magical arts of goofiness. Making balloon animals, joggling balls and bowling pins. making goofy faces with your friends and laughing as hard as you can. Most importantly, it's about realizing even the smallest amount love can have the greatest impact. The school was built to honor a young boy named Bennie, who dreamed of becoming a clown, so he could bring spread so much love to other children who were sick. A place where children and adults of every age could be silly, goofy, brave, and happy. Every day is a special day at the Clown Academy, where **love** truly is the best medicine.

Lindsey and her friends, the teachers all had their clothes on inside out, makeup on, and were all smiles waiting patiently for their special and beloved, Principal Ronnie SnotRocket. There was a large box in the center of the room, Lindsey volunteered to push the big button... *"POP"* came out balloons and a big man with purple hair, brown eyes, big red shoes, a very, very red nose and the biggest smile you've ever seen." Hi kids! Who's ready to have the best time E..verrrr…Ahh Chew!' Principal SnotRocket blew his nose so loudly whipped cream came out. All the children gathered around Principal SnotRocket spoke to them.

"Kids, behind every red nose, there is a beautiful smile to show, behind every laugh, joy is being shared. Behind every good or sad day, there is always a special hug waiting for all of us. It is not always about being the best clown, or person, it is always about being the best, YOU! "Be brave, be goofy, laugh like no one's watching. Embrace a smile, give a hug, we are all special, most importantly, I am so proud of you, guys. You make this school and this world better beyond measure. I LOVE YOU! "
Now, please stand, red noses on, and let us recite the official Clown pledge, written on the wall...

"There's Only One Kind of Special and That Is You!"

" Let us put on the Best Show, EVER!" Said Principal SnotRocket, tripping over his very long handkerchief. The children were rolling on the floor, laughing.

"There is Only One Kind Of Special AND That is You"

Lindsey
watching
the show

A-a Chew

Hello!
Kids

Principal
Snotrocket
Blowing
Bubble Gum

Happy Students

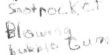

Students

Mr. Pickles
Juggling balls

Kids Riding
Bubbles
the story

At home, Lindsey her told mom and her superhero little brother, Elmer, how much she loved school. "It was MAGICAL, but the best was practicing blowing up balloons to make balloon animals." said Lindsey, happily.

"I am so happy for you, sweetie. Be the best you can be." said Mom, clearing the table after dinner. Elmer beamed with excitement, "I can't wait to GO!" said Elmer. Joyfully.

Elmer wears a red cape everywhere he goes and his best friend, Nemo their three-legged dog is always by his side. Later that night, after Lindsey took her medicine, Elmer came into the room, his arms stretched out pretending he could fly.

"Super Elmer ready for sleepy town, AWAY!" he said, flying towards Lindsey and Nemo, laying on the bed. Snuggling together for bed.

Softly, Lindsey began to sing….

"You are beautiful, you are sweet.
I love tickling your feet, red noses glow.
Do you see the rainbow?
Don't be afraid, love is here to stay,
You are beautiful, you are sweet, that why you have a beautiful heartbeat."

Lindsey hugged Elmer, kissed Nemo softly. Soon all three were fast asleep.

Elmer's
Room

Super Elmer and Super Nemo

Closet

TV

Super
Rug

dresser

desk

NEmo's and Elmen's bed

Elmer's
Toy Box

Pic Ture

That night, Lindsey had a dream where she was preforming for the children at hospital. Juggling balls and riding a unicycle on stage. "Easy, you can do this!" she told herself quietly. Lindsey rolled out on her unicycle, the children were chanting her name, "Lindsey, Yay, Lindsey." She rode around the stage on her unicycle then demonstrating her skills, but when she started juggling balls in the air, she fumbled off the unicycle and gently sat down.

"I'm sorry, I can't…" said Lindsey ready to go behind the curtain.
"You're doing fine. Keep going." said a boy from the audience.
Lindsey looked out at the audience and recognized someone's red cape; it was Elmer.

"Hi, Sis, Need Me?" Lindsey was surprised, yet happy to see her best friend.
"Elmer? What are doing here?" asked Lindsey sitting on the steps. "That's Super Elmer, I am always on duty, awake or sleepy town dreamland. Just like buzz Lightyear."

Lindsey looked at the crowd, all the kids were sound sleep. "Don't be nervous. Just have fun. You are the strongest sister I have and there is nobody funnier, more loving clown than you. I love you. When my favorite heroes, Captain Spaghetti and his sidekick, One-eyed Meatball get in a jam, they gently fight back with courage, or eat themselves, silly. Always be you because The Rainbow's Light will forever see you through." said, Super Elmer who very badly needed a cookie.

Lindsey and Elmer walked off stage and went around the room making sure everyone was in their sleeping bags. "Super Elmer and Lindsey to sleepy town away…Right after a chocolate chip cookie."

Lindsey kissed Elmer, "Thank you so much. I love you beyond measure little brother. You're my favorite superhero." Lindsey felt better and was ready to practice hard to become the best clown she could be.

LINDSEY's DREAM

Lindsey
practicing
her
Routine

Super
Elmer
Saves
Lindsey

The next day, Lindsey and her classmates worked hard perfecting their clowning techniques. "Every clown has to have good balance and a big hearty laugh like Spongebob. When riding a unicycle and trying to balance banana cream pies. You are going to fall down many times, but that's all right. Practice, take your time and keep going. I've you and we've got each other. That counts the most." said Mr. Pickles, guiding his students to start their exercises.

Lindsey practiced riding a unicycle and her balloon animal skills,
 "This is hard!" Lindsey flattened all her balloons; she gave herself a pie in the face.
Lindsey didn't laugh, she watched her friends master their clowning skills.

"Whoa wee whoa, that was close." said Mickey Juiceberry getting off his unicycle.
"Are you okay, Lindsey?" asked Nickey Juiceberry, the flying acrobat.
"It is hard to balance pies and ride at the same time." said Lindsey discouraged.
"Awe, don't worry, you'll get it." said Nickey, encouragingly.
"Why don't you come over tonight, we'll help you practice and bring Elmer along. Nickey said happily.
 "Thank you so much, guys. That would be wonderful!" Lindsey said happily.
"Of Course, you've got you." said Mickey waiting for his little brother, Pinkey
"Amazing Job today, everyone. I am proud of you! Tomorrow is goofy faces day. Practice, practice."
"Oh, NO, I can't find my whoopee cushion?" Screamed Pinky, franticly looking around.

Suddenly, there was a loud whistling sound coming from Mr. Pickles' s chair cushion
 The kids started chuckling.
 "Found It!" whispered Nicky smiling at his trick.
Mr. Pickle's face was redder than a tomato on a hot day. "Nicalie Juiceberry! How many times have I told you put this away before bubbles come out of my nose, again!" Mr. Pickles said, angrily.

 "Yes Sir!" Nickey took the whoopee cushion and ran to catch up with his friends.

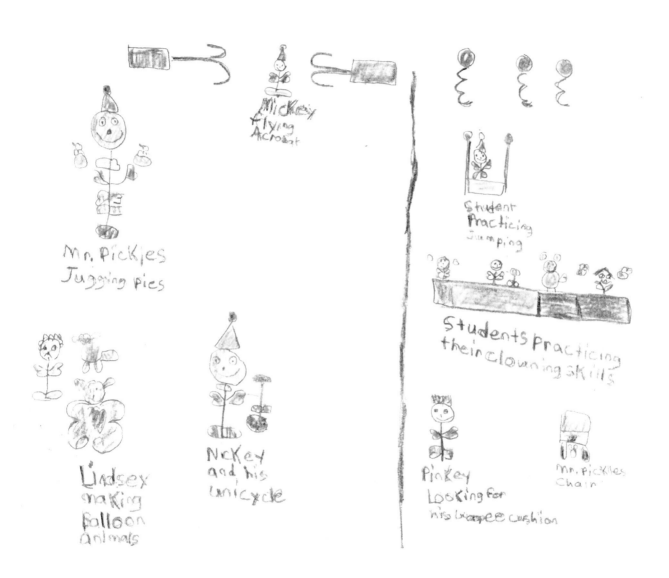

Mr. Pickjes
Jugging Pies

Mickey
Flying
Acrobat

Student
Practicing
Jumping

Students Practicing
their clowning skills

Lindsey
making
balloon
animals

Nckey
and his
unicycle

Pinkey
Looking for
his whoopee cushion

Mr. Pickles
Chair

13

When Lindsey and Elmer arrived at the Juiceberry's house, you can tell they are a circus family. You see balloon animals everywhere, a trampoline in the middle of the room. Their basement was a circus ring, where they practiced all their acts.

"I love this PLACE!" Elmer said, mesmerized by excitement. Pinky helped Elmer with his makeup. "I feel like a true clown, now!" said Elmer confidently. Lindsey followed both Mickey and Nickey downstairs to the den for circus training.

"Just take your time, focus. Forget everything else." Mickey said, smilingly. Lindsey rode around joggling with Nickey and Mickey close behind. "You're doing an excellent job!" said Nickey encouragingly. Lindsey remembered the first time she met Nickey and Mickey. When they were younger, the boys would volunteer with their parents at the hospital, to cheer up the patients by juggling and telling silly jokes. It was then, Lindsey felt inspired to become a clown to help cheer up other children going through challenging times. Overtime, all of them became best friends. Lindsey practiced hard into the night. "Thank you so much, guys, for your help. It means a lot." Lindsey said gratefully. There were pictures of the Juiceberrys on the wall, but one caught Lindsey's eye. Their dad was holding a little boy in his arms.

"He looks familiar?" said Lindsey looking closely at the picture.
She saw writing below the picture, it read simply.
"There is Only One Kind of Special and That is You!" Lindsey's eyes Beamed…
" Wait, a minute, that's Principal SnotRocket!"

"Yeah, he's our stepfather and Bennie was our stepbrother."
It all began to make sense, Principal SnotRocket had adopted the boys and they became a family.

Elmer's
Room

Super Elmer and Super Nemo

Closet

TV

Super
Rug

dresser

desk

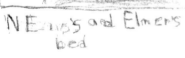

Nemo's and Elmen's
bed

Puzzel & Game

Elmer's
Toal Box

Be You

PicTure

The Juiceberrys
family portrait

"There is
Only one
Kind Of
Special and
that is You!"

Candy Machine

Chocolate
Bunny

Candy

Game Area

Elmer
Loves
Playing
HERE!

Nickey the
Flying Acrobat

mickey
guiding
Lindsey

Lindsey
balancing
books on
her head

Before Lindsey and friends graduate from the Clown Academy. Before every graduation, tts put on a show for the children at the hospital, so they can be themselves. Lindsey and her friends helped decorate the waiting room into circus mania. Clown cars, gum balls machines and stuffed animals everywhere. A special night filled with excitement, magic, jumbo belly laughs, and makin many wonderful memories to be cherished for a lifetime. The children dressed in their pajamas, a familiar, booming enthusiastic voice filled the room with wonder and excitement. The children gathered up front towards the stage. They opened their eyes in amazement.

A big banner hung high below the ceiling," Fun Under the Big Top" Principal SnotRocket dressed in his clown suit came out behind the curtain and addressed the audience. "ATTENTION: Boys, Girls, and Children of all ages. Welcome to the Clown Academy Circus! Who's ready for… AHH CHEWW!" When Principal SnotRocket sneezed, and a butterfly flew out his nose. The kids laughed as the show took off. Lindsey, Nickey, Mickey, and Pinkey rolled out on stage on their unicycles, making balloon animals, while joggling bananas cream pies in the air. The kids were beaming with big smiles watching and beamed when they got in on the act. It was a very wonderful time had by all.

THE Clown
ACADEMY CIRCUS

Flying Nickex

Pinkey

mickey   Lindsey

Happy Children and Nemo

Friends having fun

18

The Show Goes ON!

Nickey

Bowling Pins

Bowling Pins

Lindsey

Ah chew

heart tree where wishes are made

Chris

Pinky Elmer

mickey

Klye

Lily and her bear

Frieda enjoying the Smell

Happy Parents Proud of their kids

Mickey and Nickey threw balloon animals into the audience for the children to catch.

"I Got a Dog!" Screamed Kyle, jumping up and down.

"I Got a Rabbit!" Yelled Cindy.

Lindsey joggled bowling pins covered with banana cream filling and whipped cream. Lindsey enjoyed falling and covering the children in whipped cream. "Yummy, this is THE BEST SHOW EVER!" The kids laughed and screamed all night long, taking rides in the clown car and eating treats all night long. Principal SnotRocket was being silly as can be, trying to get the children to throw a pie into his face,

"I Got Youuuuu, Ronnie!" said Cindy

"You sure did sweetie, come here." Ronnie said happily, chasing after her and her friends all over. Elmer loved getting his faced painted by Pinkey. "I look Good!" said Elmer ecstatically looking in the mirror. Mickey and Nickey each gave the children rides inside the clown car. "I Love honking the horn." said Lucy beyond excited.

Mr. and Mrs. Pickles gave all the students piggyback rides and hugs.

All the children had a wonderful time, as the evening wined down, Ronnie hugged all his children.

"Amazing Job, guys! I am so proud of all of you! I love you beyond measure."

"Thank you, Dad. We love you more." Pinkey hugging his father goodnight.

"Thank you so much for all your help, I couldn't have done it without you." Lindsey told both Mickey and Nickey.

"Awe, don't mention it, we were happy to help. You were amazing out there!" said Mickey and Nickey together.

"This was the most fun I've had in a long tong time." Lindsey told her mom.

"It was amazing, bubbles. Now, get some rest, tomorrow is Graduation Day!" said mom kissing her goodnight.

21

The day has finally come for Lindsey and her friends to graduate from the Clown Academy. Lindsey's mom and brother took their seat on the lawn with the other families, waiting for their loved ones to walk out and receive their official red nose. Tears began to flow as Principal SnotRocket addressed the audience.

"Family, friends, children of all ages, thank you all so much for coming on this beautiful day, welcoming the newest graduating class of the Clown Academy. All of you have worked so hard, remaining strong and dedicated to your studies, never losing your bright and infectious personalitie through difficult and challenging moments. You kept going, inspiring yourselves and all those around you. I could not be prouder of all of you. I have been a professional clown educator for fort five years, and I continue to be to be inspired by the power of compassion. Love truly is the best medicine of all. The academy is stronger because of you. Thank you! I love you! Principal SnotRocket wiped his nose and presented each student with their official Red Nose, along with a Giant Hug.

"Adam Appletown,
Lindsey Crickethopper,
Michael Juiceberry,
Nicalie Juiceberry,
Patrick "Pinky" Juiceberry,"

"Congratulations guys, you can now call yourselves, Professional Clowns." The students honked their noses in excitement. "I'm so proud of you!" said mom hugging her tightly. "Thank you, mom" Elmer climbed onto Lindsey shoulders. "You did it! Now, it's my turn!" said Elmer wearing his sister's new nose. Suddenly, a loud cry came from the sky. It was Pinkey, high above the clouds, he had accidently released the rope. Soon, Pinky, his whoopie cushion were floating away. "Mickey chuckled, "Here, we go again!" "We're coming, Pinky!" said, Nickey running at high speed to catch up to Pinky and the balloon. Lindsey looked at Elmer "Ready?" Elmer put on Lindsey's red nose and beamed, "Let's GO!" Lindsey and Elmer joined them, Pinkey was rescued safe and sound. Remembering this special message along the way...

"There is Only One Kind of Special and that is You!"

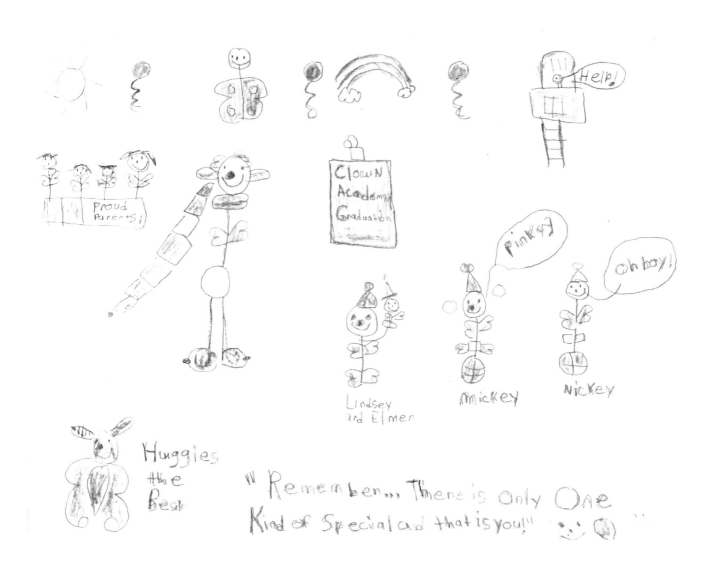

Super Elmer's Offical Superhero Pledge

I AM ME…
I always try to be brave and kind.
I try to help others in need.
I am a friend to all animals and insects, especially worms and bedbugs.
I give all my love to my family, friends, teachers, pets, frults and vegetables.
I AM ME….
I might be small, but I am strong and tall.
I will make mistakes and I will fall, but that is a special lesson for us all.
I try to give all of my heart to everyone around me. There is always more to be
There's only one kind of special and that is Me, and that is all I strive to be.

Be You
Love Lindsey and Elmer

The End

YOUR SUPERHERO PLEDGE

Made in United States
North Haven, CT
19 October 2021

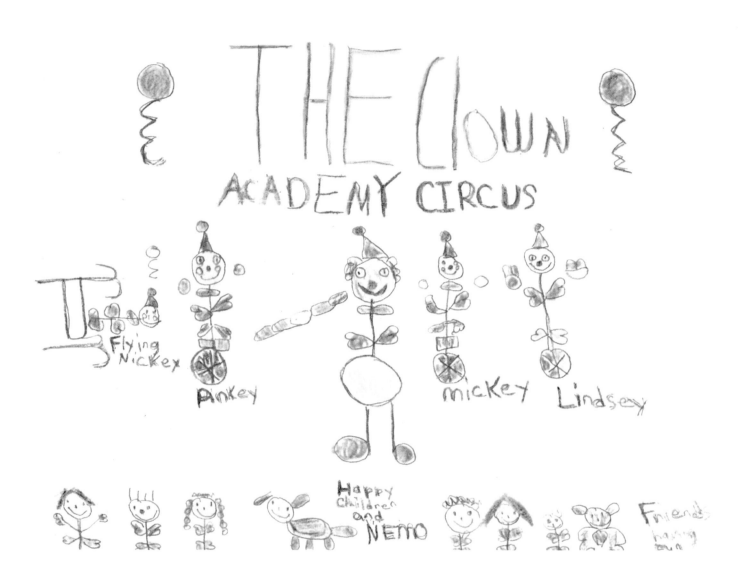

THE Clown
ACADEMY CIRCUS

Flying
Nickex

Pinkey

mickey   Lindsey

Happy
Children
and
Nemo

Friends
having

18

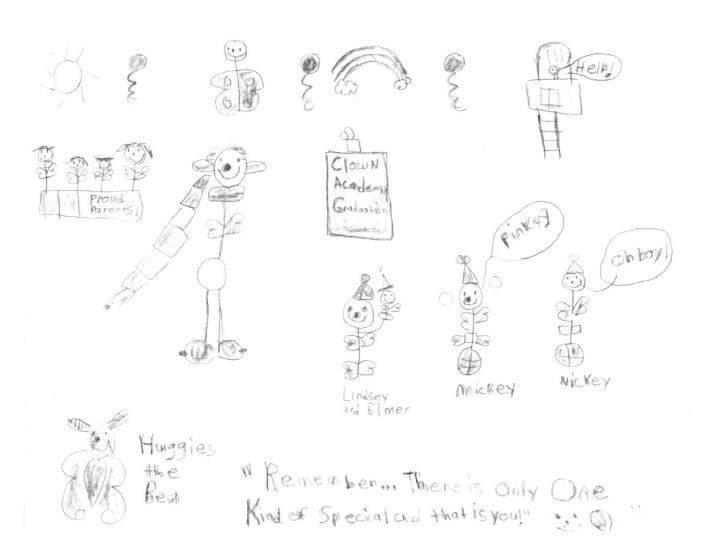

23

Made in United States
North Haven, CT
19 October 2021